D1401335

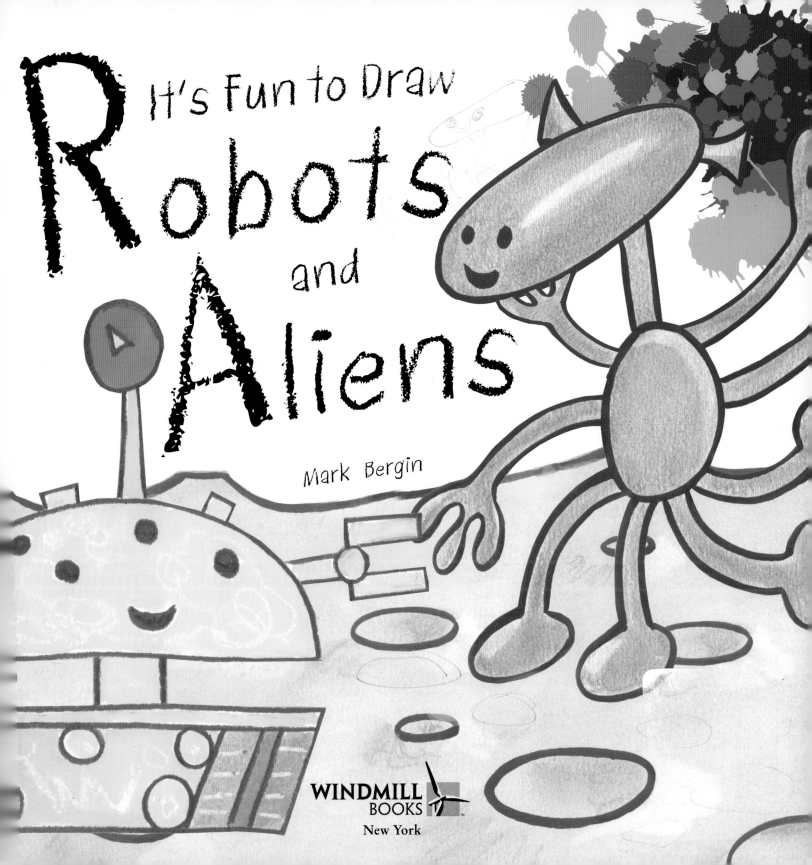

It's Fun to Draw
Robots
and
Aliens

Mark Bergin

WINDMILL BOOKS

New York

Published in 2012 by Windmill Books, LLC
303 Park Avenue South, Suite #1280, New York, NY 10010-3657

Editor: Rob Walker
U.S. Editor: Sara Antill

Library of Congress Cataloging-in-Publication Data

Bergin, Mark.
 Robots and aliens / by Mark Bergin. — 1st ed.
     p. cm. — (It's fun to draw)
 Includes index.
 ISBN 978-1-61533-353-0 (library binding)
1. Androids in art—Juvenile literature. 2. Extraterrestrial beings in art—Juvenile literature. 3. Drawing—Technique—Juvenile literature. I. Title.

NC825.A53B47 2012
743'.87—dc22

2010052108

Manufactured in Heshan, China

CPSIA Compliance Information: Batch #SS1102WM:
For Further Information contact Windmill Books, New York,
New York at 1-866-478-0556

Contents

Klank, a Robot

1 Draw a rectangle for the head. Add a mouth, ears, and dots for the eyes.

2 Draw the neck and a rectangle for the body.

You Can Do It!

Use a black felt-tip pen for the lines. Then add color with colored felt-tip pens.

3 Draw the legs. Add circles for the knee joints.

4 Add the arms and hands, with circles at the elbow joints.

Claude, an Alien

1 Start with the head and body.

2 Add one big eye and a belly button.

4 Draw wobbly arms and hands.

Splat-a-Fact!
Asteroids are small, rocky bodies in space. They circle the Sun as Earth does.

3 Add the feet and three toes.

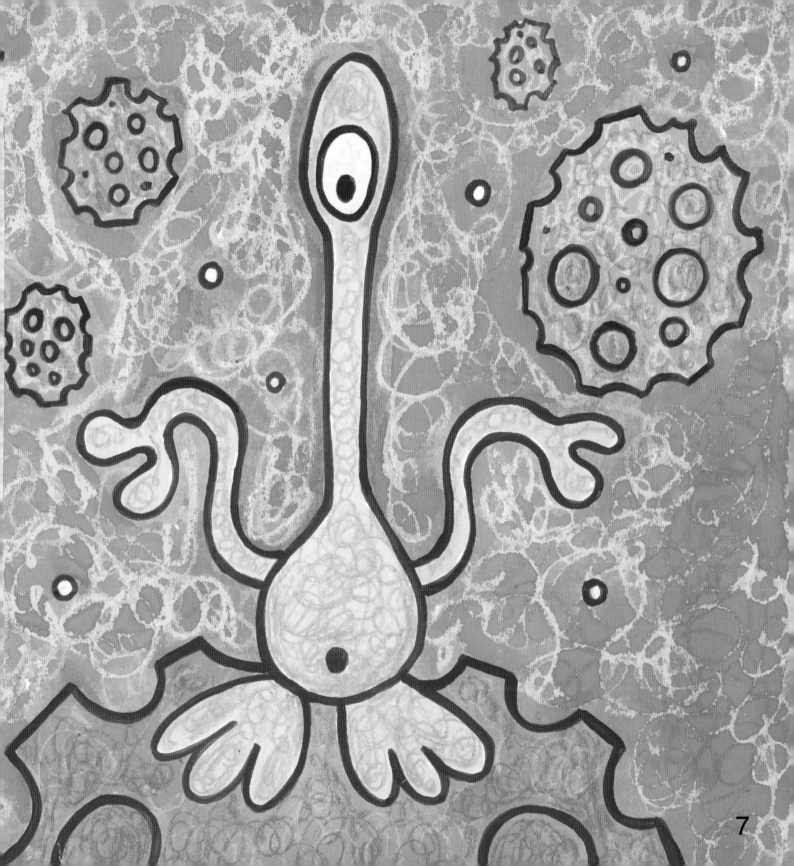

spike, an Alien

You Can Do It!

Use a dark pencil to draw the outline and add color with watercolor paint.

1

Start with a spiky shape for the head.

2 Add a smiley mouth and four dots for eyes.

Splat-a-Fact!

Scientists say there are active volcanoes on the surface of the planet Venus.

4 Add five legs and feet.

3 Draw the skin pattern.

8

Bob the Blob,
an Alien

You Can Do It!
Use oil pastels. Blend or smudge them with your fingers. Use a felt-tip pen for the lines.

1 Start with the body.

Splat-a-Fact!
Your skeleton gives your body its basic shape. Without it, you'd be a blob, too!

2 Draw two big feet.

3 Add the antennae with eyes at the ends.

4 Draw one big eye and a mouth.

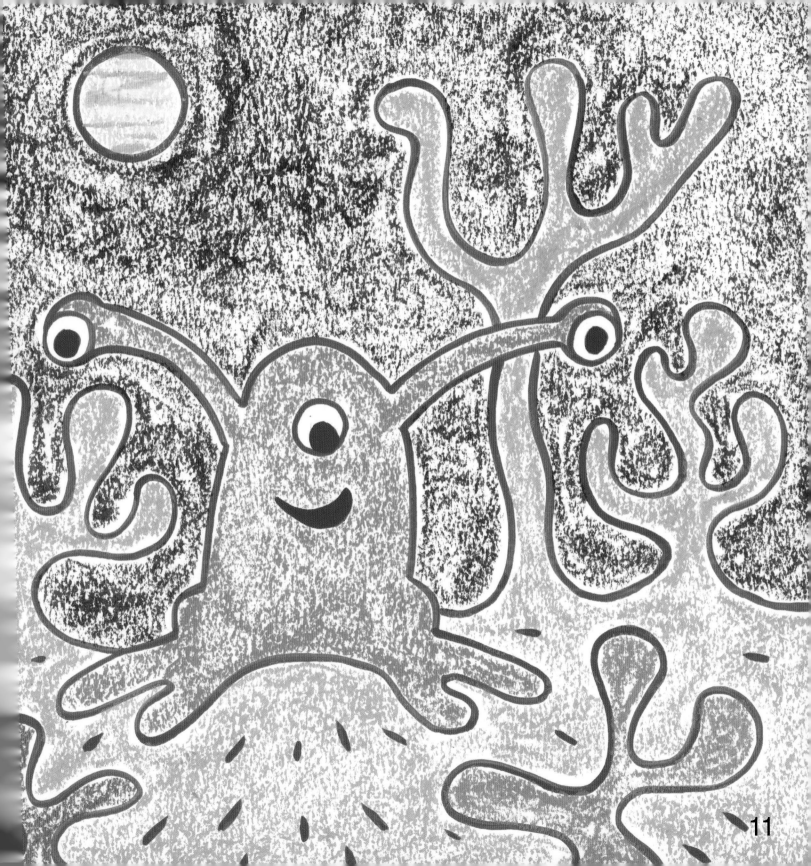

Rivet, a Robot

1 Start with a circle for the body. Draw a line near the top and add details.

2 Add the mouth and dots for eyes.

3 Draw the legs and feet with circles and half circles.

You Can Do It!

Use a black felt-tip pen for the lines. Add color by dabbing on paint with a sponge.

4 Draw a glass helmet.

5 Add circles for the arms. Draw the hands.

Splat-a-Fact!

Most robots today are just jointed arms.

13

Grabbit, a Robot

1 Tear the head and body shapes out of paper. Glue the body and head down on another sheet of paper. Add a mouth, a line, and eyes.

2 Tear out the shape for the flashing light. Glue it down.

Splat-a-Fact!

We can use robots to do jobs in places that are too dangerous for people.

You Can Do It!

Tear the robot's shapes out of colored paper. Glue them to a sheet of colored paper. Use a felt-tip pen for the face and flashing light.

3 Tear out shapes for the legs and feet. Glue them to the paper.

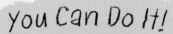

4 Tear out shapes for the arms, hands, and a red rock. Glue them down.

15

Octo, an Alien

1 Start with a big oval for the head and a small oval for the body. Draw two lines for the neck.

2 Add the ears, mouth, and dots for the eyes.

You Can Do It!

Use colored pastels. Blend the colors with your finger. Draw the lines with a felt-tip pen.

3 Draw four legs and feet.

Splat-a-Fact!

There are animals on Earth with eight limbs, too. Spiders, octopuses, and scorpions all have eight legs.

4 Add four arms and four hands.

16

Rover, a Robot

1 Start with a big semicircle for the head. Add a face.

2 Add the shape of the tracks. Join the tracks to the head.

You Can Do It!
Add texture with a white crayon. Then paint over your picture with watercolor paint. Use a felt-tip pen to draw lines.

3 Add lines and circles to the tracks.

4 Draw the arms and antennae.

Martian Mike, an Alien

1 Start with a triangular shape for the head. Add the small, round body and neck.

2 Add the eyes, mouth, and antennae.

you Can Do It!
Use crayons to create texture and paint over it with watercolor paint. Use a felt-tip pen for the outlines.

Splat-a-Fact!
People sometimes refer to aliens as "little green men."

3 Add the legs and feet.

4 Draw the arms and hands.

Rusty, a Robot

1 Draw a circle for the head. Add the eyes and mouth.

2 Add the body and the neck.

You Can Do It!

Use a black felt-tip pen for the lines and use different colors of felt-tip pens to color in the rest of the picture.

Splat-a-Fact!

Computers control robots in the same way your brain controls your body.

4 Draw the arms and hands. Add circles at the elbow and wrist joints.

3 Draw the shapes for the legs and feet. Add cicles at the knee joints.

5 Finish off the head.

22

Zango, an Alien

1 Start with an oval for the body. Add five antennae.

2 Add five eyes and a mouth.

You Can Do It!

Use a black felt-tip pen for the lines. Add color with colored pencils.

Splat-a-Fact!

The snails that you might find in a garden have eyes on the ends of stalks, as Zango does.

3 Draw six legs and feet using curved lines and semicircles.

4 Add a big semicircle for the flying saucer. Add details.

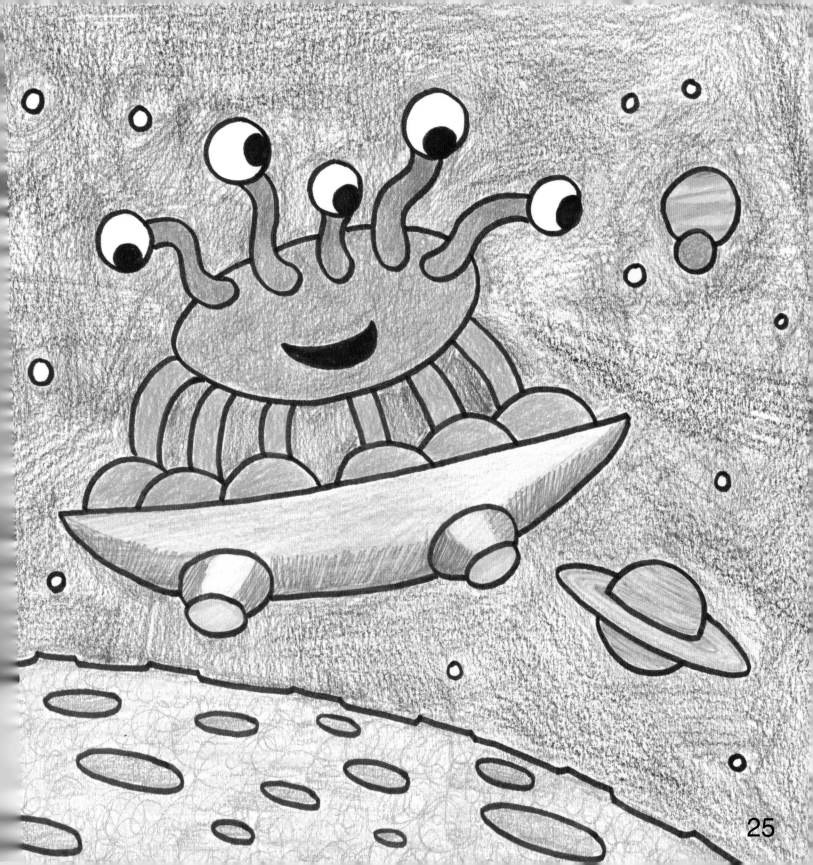

Zakk, an Alien

1 Start with ovals for the head and body. Add the neck.

2 Draw ears, a mouth, and five eyes.

You Can Do It!

Use a felt-tip pen for the lines. Add color using oil pastels in a scribbly way to create textures.

Splat-a-Fact!

Superman, E.T., Yoda, and Mr. Spock are all alien characters you may have seen in movies.

3 Draw the legs with curvy lines.

4 Add two tentacle arms with curvy lines.

27

Mega-Klank, a Robot

1 Cut out a rectangle for the head. Glue it to a piece of paper. Draw the eyes and mouth.

You Can Do It!
Cut out the robot shapes from colored paper. Glue them onto a sheet of blue paper as shown. Use a felt-tip pen for the lines.

2 Cut out rectangles for the body and neck. Glue down the neck and the body.

3 Cut out the leg shapes. Glue them down. Add a line with a felt-tip pen. Cut out foot shapes and glue them down.

4 Cut out the shapes of the arms. Glue them down. Cut out shapes for details. Glue them down.

Make sure you get an adult to help you when using scissors!

Splat-a-Fact!
Robots are machines, so they don't sleep.

Whizz-Pop, a Robot

2 Cut out shapes for the body. Glue them into place.

1 Cut out the shape of the head. Glue it down. Add the eyes and mouth with a marker pen.

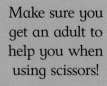

Make sure you get an adult to help you when using scissors!

You Can Do It!

Cut the robot shapes out of tin foil. Glue them onto a sheet of black paper. Use a marker pen for the lines. Add paint splatters and torn paper for the background.

3 Cut out shapes for the feet and the head details. Add lines with a marker pen.

4 Cut out shapes for the arms and hands. Glue them down. Add circles at the joints with a marker pen.

Splat-a-Fact!
R2-D2, the Cylons, and the Transformers are popular robot characters.

Read More

Bergin, Mark. *How to Draw Robots*. How to Draw. New York: PowerKids Press, 2009.

Bridgeman, Roger. *Robot*. New York: DK Children, 2004.

Davis, Barbara J. *The Kids' Guide to Aliens*. Mankato, MN: Capstone Press, 2009.

Glossary

antennae (an-TEH-nee) Thin, rodlike feelers on the heads of certain animals.

circuit (SER-ket) The complete path of an electric current.

joint (JOYNT) A place where a leg and arm can bend, such as the knee and the elbow.

smudge (SMUJ) To blend together.

tentacles (TEN-tih-kulz) Long, thin growths used to touch, hold, or move that are usually on the head or near the mouths of animals.

texture (TEKS-chur) How something feels when you touch it.

Index

Web Sites

For Web resources related to the subject of this book,
go to: www.windmillbooks.com/weblinks and select this book's title.